Summer
HOT DAYS OUT IN THE SUN!

By LISA BELL

Illustrated by EMILY BROOKS

CANTATA
LEARNING
MANKATO, MINNESOTA

WWW.CANTATALEARNING.COM

CANTATA LEARNING

MANKATO, MINNESOTA

Published by Cantata Learning
1710 Roe Crest Drive
North Mankato, MN 56003
www.cantatalearning.com

Library of Congress Control Number: 2014957000
978-1-63290-266-5 (hardcover/CD)
978-1-63290-418-8 (paperback/CD)
978-1-63290-460-7 (paperback)

Summer: Hot Days Out in the Sun! by Lisa Bell
Illustrated by Emily Brooks

Book design, Tim Palin Creative
Editorial direction, Flat Sole Studio
Executive musical production and direction, Elizabeth Draper
Music arranged and produced by Mark Oblinger

Printed in the United States of America.

VISIT
WWW.CANTATALEARNING.COM/ACCESS-OUR-MUSIC
TO SING ALONG TO THE SONG

Summer is the season between spring and fall. It is the warmest season. The sun is in the sky most of the day.

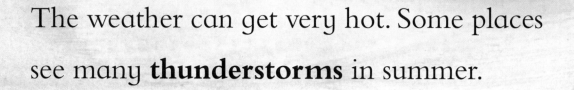

The weather can get very hot. Some places
see many **thunderstorms** in summer.

Now turn the page, and sing along.

Summertime, summer fun,
hot days out in the sun!

We play all day. We're never done!
Summertime, summer fun!

Morning **breezes** and skies of blue

turn into a stormy afternoon or two.

Thunder claps and rain falls

during the hottest season of them all.

Dressing when it's hot is quick.
Shorts and sandals do the trick!

A bathing suit and garden hose
can keep you cool from head to toes!

Summertime, summer fun,
hot days out in the sun!

We play all day. We're never done!
Summertime, summer fun.

Our part of Earth **tilts** toward the sun,
bringing warmth to everyone.

Animals find **shade** to keep cool.
People cool off in swimming pools!

Summer brings tasty **bounties**
from farms out in the country.

Tomatoes, peppers, corn, and beans.

Peaches, berries, and nectarines.

At **dusk** we come home from the park.

Then we catch fireflies in the dark.

18

The crickets **chirp**. The stars are bright
on a magical summer night!

Summertime, summer fun,
hot days out in the sun!

We play all day. We're never done!

Summertime, summer fun.

SONG LYRICS
Summer: Hot Days Out in the Sun!

Summertime, summer fun,
hot days out in the sun!

We play all day. We're never done!
Summertime, summer fun!

Morning breezes and skies of blue
turn into a stormy afternoon or two.

Thunder claps and rain falls
during the hottest season of them all.

Dressing when it's hot is quick.
Shorts and sandals do the trick!

A bathing suit and garden hose
can keep you cool from head to toes!

Summertime, summer fun,
hot days out in the sun!

We play all day. We're never done!
Summertime, summer fun.

Our part of Earth tilts toward the sun,
bringing warmth to everyone.

Animals find shade to keep cool.
People cool off in swimming pools!

Summer brings tasty bounties
from farms out in the country.

Tomatoes, peppers, corn, and beans.
Peaches, berries, and nectarines.

At dusk we come home from the park.
Then we catch fireflies in the dark.

The crickets chirp, the stars are bright
on a magical summer night!

Summertime, summer fun,
hot days out in the sun!

We play all day. We're never done!
Summertime, summer fun.

Summer: Hot Days Out in the Sun!

Mark Oblinger

Chorus

Sum-mer-time, sum-mer fun, hot days out in the sun! We play all day. We're nev-er done! Sum-mer-time, sum-mer fun!

Verse

1. Morn-ing breez-es and skies of blue turn in-to a storm-y af-ter-noon or two.

Thun-der claps and rain falls dur-ing the hot-test sea-son of them all.

Verse 2

Dressing when it's hot is quick.
Shorts and sandals do the trick!
A bathing suit and garden hose
can keep you cool from head to toes!

Chorus

Summertime, summer fun,
hot days out in the sun!
We play all day. We're never done!
Summertime, summer fun!

Verse 3

Our part of Earth tilts toward the sun,
bringing warmth to everyone.
Animals find shade to keep cool.
People cool off in swimming pools!

Verse 4

Summer brings tasty bounties
from farms out in the country.
Tomatoes, peppers, corn, and beans.
Peaches, berries, and nectarines.

Bridge

At dusk we come home from the park. Then we catch fire-flies in the dark. The crick-ets chirp. The

stars are bright on a mag-i-cal sum-mer night!

Chorus

Summertime, summer fun,
hot days out in the sun!
We play all day. We're never done!
Summertime, summer fun!

GLOSSARY

bounties—large amounts of food gathered from crops

breezes—gentle winds

chirp—a short, light sound a cricket makes

dusk—the time of day right after sunset when it is almost dark

shade—an area out of the sun

thunderstorms—storms with rain, lighting, and thunder

tilts—leans to one side or is not straight

GUIDED READING ACTIVITIES

1. Who is this author of this book? Why do you think she picked the title Summer? Can you think of other titles for the book?

2. What are some of your favorite summer activities? Are any of them shown in this story?

3. In three sentences or less, write a summary of this book.

TO LEARN MORE

DeGezelle, Terri. *Exploring Summer.* Mankato, MN: Capstone, 2012.

Herrington, Lisa M. *How Do You Know It's Summer?* New York: Scholastic, 2014.

Smith, Siân. *What Can You See in Summer?* Chicago, IL: Capstone-Heinemann Library, 2015.

Yee, Wong Herbert. *Summer Days and Nights.* New York: Henry Holt, 2012.